O9-ABH-862

THE
QUOTIDIAN MYSTERIES

THE
QUOTIDIAN MYSTERIES

Laundry, Liturgy and "Women's Work"

KATHLEEN NORRIS

1998 Madeleva Lecture
in Spirituality

PAULIST PRESS
New York / Mahwah, N.J.

The Publisher gratefully acknowledges use of the following: "The Bath" by Laura Gilpin, which first appeared in *Poetry*. Copyright 1984 by The Modern Poetry Association. Reprinted by permission of the Editor of *Poetry*. Quotation from "An Easter Lily," copyright 1994 by Anne Porter, from *An Altogether Different Language*, Zoland Books, Inc., Cambridge, Massachusetts. "Making Salad" by Margaret Gibson. Reprinted by permission of Louisiana State University Press from *Out in the Open*, by Margaret Gibson. Copyright 1989 by Margaret Gibson. "Housecleaning," an excerpt from "Persephone," and one from "Ascension" are from *Little Girls in Church*, by Kathleen Norris, copyright 1995. Reprinted by permission of the University of Pittsburgh Press.

Cover design by Moe Berman

This lecture was adapted from the author's forthcoming book in progress, to be published by Riverhead Books. Published by arrangement with the author and Riverhead Books. All rights reserved. For information or permission to excerpt from this book contact: Riverhead Books, a part of Penguin Putnam, Inc., 200 Madison Avenue, New York, NY 10016.

Library of Congress Cataloging-in-Publication Data

Norris, Kathleen, 1947–
    The quotidian mysteries : laundry, liturgy and "women's work"
/ Kathleen Norris.
        p. cm. — (Madeleva lecture in spirituality ; 1998)
    Includes bibliographical references.
    ISBN 0-8091-3801-8 (alk. paper)
    1. Women—Religious life. 2. Spiritual life—Christianity. 3.
Norris, Kathleen, 1947–   . I. Title. II. Series.
BV4526.2.N675   1998
248.8′43—dc21   98-9949
                                                        CIP

Published by Paulist Press
997 Macarthur Boulevard
Mahwah, New Jersey 07430

Printed and bound in the
United States of America

TIDIAN MYSTERIES *The Quotid*
ian Mysteries The Quotidian Mysteries THE
QUOTIDIAN MYSTERIES THE
QUOTIDIAN MYSTERIES THE QUOTIDI
AN MYSTERIES *The Quotidian*
Mysteries The Quotidian Mysteries THE QU
OTIDIAN MYSTERIES THE QUOTIDI
AN MYSTERIES THE QUOTIDIAN
MYSTERIES *The Quotidian Mysteri*
es The Quotidian Mysteries THE QUOTID
IAN MYSTERIES THE QUOTIDIAN MYST
ERIES THE QUOTIDIAN MYST
ERIES *The Quotidian Mysteries* The
Quotidian Mysteries THE QUOTIDIAN
MYSTERIES THE QUOTIDIAN MYSTERIES
THE QUOTIDIAN MYSTERI
ES *The Quotidian Mysteries* The Quotidian
Mysteries THE QUOTIDIAN MYS-
TERIES THE QUOTIDIAN MYSTERIES THE

To my mother and father

Quotidian: occurring every day; belonging to every day; commonplace, ordinary.

(*Merriam-Webster Third New International Dictionary*)

Let us remember that the life in which we ought to be interested is "daily" life. We can, each of us, only call the present time our own....Our Lord tells us to pray for today, and so he prevents us from tormenting ourselves about tomorrow. It is as if [God] were to say to us: "[It is I] who gives you this day [and] will also give you what you need for this day. [It is I] who makes the sun to rise. [It is I] who scatters the darkness of night and reveals to you the rays of the sun."

—Gregory of Nyssa,
On the Lord's Prayer

THE QUOTIDIAN MYSTERIES: LAUNDRY, LITURGY AND "WOMEN'S WORK"

My introduction to the Roman Catholic world was a full immersion baptism in the heady milieu of an Irish-American wedding. The man I was dating, who later became my husband, had invited me to attend the wedding ceremony of a high-school classmate, consisting of a weekend of dinners, parties and, of course, church. It was one of our first dates, a fact that now seems rich with God's good humor. David and I took a train from New York City to the far reaches of Long Island, and I soon found myself in the midst of a large Irish Catholic family—eleven children, I believe, and numerous grandchildren, cousins, aunts, uncles and family friends milling about in an atmosphere so dense, warm and lively that I felt as if I had been placed into a den of puppies. The marvelous abundance and seemingly bottomless hospitality were overwhelming to my timid Protestant soul—the feasting! the drinking! the toddlers, dogs and cats contending for scraps underneath the picnic

1

tables at the family potluck the night before the wedding! Enough for everyone; more than enough. Amazing.

At the time—this was 1973—the Christian religion seemed a part of my past, something I had put aside when I went to college just a few years before. I had not been to any religious services for years, except when visiting my grandparents in South Dakota, and while I enjoyed accompanying my grandmother to church and especially singing Protestant hymns, worship itself held little meaning for me. I had seldom been to a Catholic mass, and never as an adult. Thus, during the wedding, I had very little idea of what was going on around the altar or what the ritual actions and words were supposed to signify. I was mildly curious but clueless, and my husband-to-be and his friends were too hung-over to be of much help. They were mostly "lapsed" Catholics like my husband, the products of parochial schools in the 1950s and Jesuit colleges in the 1960s. They seemed vastly bored by the proceedings and had not gone forward to receive communion. But I watched the ceremony intently from far back in the big stone church. And at one point, I gasped. "Look," I said, tugging on David's sleeve. "Look at that! The priest is cleaning up! He's doing the dishes!" My husband shrugged; others in the pew looked at me and then at him, as if to say—Dave, your girl-friend has gone soft in the head.

2

But I found it remarkable—and still find it remarkable—that in that big, fancy church, after all of the dress-up and the formalities of the wedding mass, homage was being paid to the lowly truth that we human beings must wash the dishes after we eat and drink. The chalice, which had held the very blood of Christ, was no exception. And I found it enormously comforting to see the priest as a kind of daft housewife, overdressed for the kitchen, in bulky robes, puttering about the altar, washing up after having served so great a meal to so many people. It brought the mass home to me and gave it meaning. It welcomed me, a stranger, someone who did not know the responses of the mass, or even the words of the sanctus. After the experience of a liturgy that had left me feeling disoriented, eating and drinking were something I could understand. That and the housework. This was my first image of the mass, my door in, as it were, and it has served me well for years.

But "doing the dishes" seems a risky subject for a lecture series devoted to the education and spiritual well-being of women. Those daily chores, such as gathering water, preparing food, cooking, serving and cleaning, have so consistently been considered "women's work" in so many of the world's cultures—and I can tell you it's a tradition that is alive and well where I live, in western South Dakota—that it has come to seem the root of women's oppression. A recent study of women in

3

their sixties determined that they recover more slowly than men from heart surgery because they resume their customary household duties too soon after coming home from the hospital. Part of this is due to internal pressure, the fact that so many women of their generation have found their identity in being traditional housewives. But the researchers also found that husbands and family members were unwilling to pitch in and help with the housework once a woman returned from the hospital. The husbands in particular demonstrated a remarkable unwillingness to see ordinary household tasks as anything but an exclusively female role. The desire to "let the little woman do it" prevailed, even when her health was in jeopardy.

Educating women is meant to free us from being relegated to such thoroughly domestic roles, and it does. But the daily we have always with us, a nagging reminder that the dishes must be done, the floor mopped or vacuumed, the dirty laundry washed. If we have grown in professional status so as to be busy with more important matters, or simply if we have enough money, we can shove the problem aside, which usually means hiring other women to do it—women who may be grateful to be employed, because they need the pay. All too often, however, we stigmatize such work as "menial," considering domestic or janitorial work to be suitable only for those who are too limited mentally to find employment elsewhere.

Cleaning up after others, or even ourselves, is not what we educate our children to do; it's for someone else's children, the less intelligent, less educated and less well-off.

But it is also the work of the priest at mass, which suggests to me that we have something worth exploring. When I looked up the word *menial* in my treasured guidebook to the history of English, Eric Partridge's *Origins,* I found myself sent to the word *manor. Menial* derives from a Latin word meaning "to remain," or "to dwell in a household." It is thus a word about connections, about family and household ties. That it has come to convey something servile, the work of servants, or even slaves, is significant. It may help to explain one of the strangest things about our culture: that in America we willingly pay the garbage collector much more in salary than we pay those who care for our infants in day-care centers. Both might be considered "menial" jobs, but the woman's work, the care of small children, is that which was once done for free—often by slaves— within the confines of the household. Precisely because it is so important, so close to us, so basic, so bound up with home and nurture, it is considered to be of less importance than that which is done in public, such as garbage collecting. This may be an example of a familiarity that has bred contempt, a kind of hubris that allows men and women alike to imagine that by devaluing the bonds that connect us to the womanly, to the household, to the daily, we can rise above them.

But not one of us can escape the daily needs that are met in family living, from the changing of a baby's diaper to the feeding of ourselves and those closest to us. The most destitute among us are the homeless, literally the household-less, and also those whose households have become unbearably lonely. Television may take the place of an extended family, providing some sense of companionship and a window into a larger world. But it is not really there in the sense that another person can be, someone who is willing to shoulder the menial household tasks that constitute no small part of ordinary daily life.

The fact that none of us can rise so far in status as to remove ourselves from the daily, bodily nature of life on this earth is not usually considered a cause for celebration, but rather the opposite. The daily routines that provide a modicum of discipline in our lives are perceived as a drag, a monotony that can occasion listlessness, apathy and despair. The word *acedia* is not much in use these days—the *American Heritage Dictionary* defines it as "spiritual torpor or apathy; ennui"—but I wonder if much of the frantic boredom and enervating depression that constitute an epidemic in modern life are not merely the ancient demon of acedia in contemporary dress. Although acedia was long thought to be the province of monastics alone, plaguing them because of the lack of distraction in their daily lives, I believe that the description of acedia given by the fourth-century monk Evagrius is as relevant to us in twentieth-century America as when it was written. He states that the bad thought, or demon, of acedia "makes it seem that the sun hardly moves, if at all, and that the day is fifty hours long. Then [it] constrains the monk to look constantly out the windows, to walk outside the cell, to gaze carefully at the sun to determine how far it stands from the ninth hour" [i.e., lunchtime].

Once the monk has given in to these outward distractions, the thought of acedia moves inward, and Evagrius writes that it "instills in the heart of the monk a hatred for the place, a hatred for his very life itself." He begins to think less of the other monks—we might translate this as our family, coworkers or neighbors—brooding on the ways they have angered, offended or merely failed to encourage him. "This demon," Evagrius reports, then drives the monk "to desire other sites where he can more easily find work and make a real success of himself." Having rejected the present and present company, the monk begins to dwell in self-pitying "[memories] of his dear ones and his former way of life." Acedia then moves in for the kill, "[depicting] life stretching out for a long period of time, and brings before the mind's eye the toil of the ascetic struggle and, as the saying has it, leaves no leaf unturned to induce the monk to forsake his cell and drop out of the fight." A friend of mine who has suffered from severe suicidal tendencies for much of her life once said that exhaustion was at the heart of it, the simple inability to bear the thought of going on.

Any person called to a vocation that is inner-directed and requires one to spend a good deal of time alone is subject to periodic attacks of acedia. The writing process is notoriously cyclical—and dangerous if one is prone to either mania or depression or both. There is the "up" of an inspired bout of writing and the "down" of seemingly fruitless labor and revisions, and times when one is incapable of writing at all. When I was a very young writer, I hungered for more, always more. But deep down, I had so little faith in myself, let alone in my vocation as a writer, that I saw each poem as potentially my last. Having invested my psychic and emotional energies in a romantic notion of "inspiration," I would panic whenever the ability to write seemed to leave me. Now, rather than succumb to despair during my dry spells, I generally employ a prairie metaphor and think of it as a lifesaver, a dying down to the roots during a drought. Although the grasses look dead, they are merely dormant, and the slightest bit of moisture will occasion a change.

For me, that life-giving moisture most often comes not from within, but through other people. I once complained to a friend, a Benedictine abbot, when he telephoned me, that things had not been going well, that I had lately been experiencing depression and acedia not as "the noonday demon" of monastic lore, but as a twenty-four-hour-a-day proposition. He sighed and said, "We are speaking of cosmic time. And it is always noon somewhere." Small comfort at the time, but I did realize that his phone call to me, out of the blue, was pure grace. His comment had made me laugh, and at myself. And in that slight moment of release I began to recognize that I might turn away from depression and embrace the hope that dispels it.

I had been feeling as if my life were a black hole—nothing but unrelenting pressure, deadlines, family business, demands on my time and my very self that threatened to swallow me up—and his call helped to break open the hard little kernel of my despair so that new life could come. I recalled the acorns I had seen not long before, on the grounds of his monastery. They carpeted the grass next to their mamas, those silent, tall, imposing oak trees. My husband and I had both commented on them—we so rarely see oak trees anymore, that they became a feast for our Dakota eyes. Now, although I was too weak to even think of feasting, I had at least remembered gratitude, which, like hope, is a force powerful enough to penetrate even the deep pit of depression. Lo and behold, out of what had seemed hopeless, utterly

9

dead, new life emerged, including this essay that you are reading.

I generally dislike the careless use of birthing imagery applied to the process of writing. The distinction that is made in the Nicene Creed is a useful one: God is a begetter, not a maker, and poets are makers, not begetters. *Maker* is what the word *poet* means at its Greek root, and I am all too acutely aware that what I make, the poems and the personae that fill them, are not creatures in the fullest sense, having life and breath. But I do detect in the quotidian, meaning daily or ordinary, rhythms of writing a stage that might be described as *parturient*, or in labor, about to produce or come forth with an idea or discovery. And it always seems that just when daily life seems most unbearable, stretching out before me like a prison sentence, when I seem most dead inside, reduced to mindlessness, bitter tears or both, that what is inmost breaks forth, and I realize that what had seemed "dead time" was actually a period of gestation.

It is a quotidian mystery that dailiness can lead to such despair and yet also be at the core of our salvation. We express this every time we utter the Lord's Prayer. As Simone Weil so eloquently stated it in her essay, "Concerning the Our Father," the "bread of this world" is all that nourishes and energizes us, not only food but the love of friends and family, "money, ambition, consideration...power...everything that puts into us the capacity for action." She reminds us that we need to keep praying for this food, acknowledging our needs as daily, because in the act of asking, the prayer awakens in us the trust that God will provide. But, like the manna that God provided to Israel in the desert, this "bread" cannot be stored. "We cannot bind our will today for tomorrow," Weil writes; "we cannot make a pact with [Christ] that tomorrow he will be within us, even in spite of ourselves." Each day brings with it not only the necessity of eating but the renewal of our love of and in God. This may sound like a simple thing, but it is not easy to maintain faith, hope or love in the everyday. I wonder if this is because human pride, and particularly a preoccupation with intellectual, artistic or spiritual matters, can provide a convenient way to ignore our ordinary, daily, bodily needs.

As a human being, Jesus Christ was as subject to the daily as any of us. And I see both the miracle of manna and incarnation of Jesus Christ as scandals. They suggest that God is intimately concerned with our very bodies and their needs, and I doubt that this is really what we want to hear. Our bodies fail us, they grow old, flabby and feeble, and eventually they lead us to the cross. How tempting it is to disdain what God has created, and to retreat into a comfortable gnosticism. The members of the Heaven's Gate cult regarded their bodies as obstacles to perfection, mere "containers" to be discarded on their way to what they called "a level beyond human." The Christian perspective could not be more different; it views the human body as our God-given means to salvation, for beyond the cross God has effected resurrection.

We want life to have meaning, we want fulfillment, healing and even ecstasy, but the human paradox is that we find these things by starting where we are, not where we wish we were. We must look for blessings to come from unlikely, everyday places—out of Galilee, as it were—and not in spectacular events, such as the coming of a comet. Although artists and poets have not been notoriously reverent in the twentieth century— Dylan Thomas, as he lay on his deathbed, is rumored to have said to the nun caring for him, "God bless you, Sister, may all your sons be archbishops"—the aesthetic sensibility is attuned to the sacramental possibility in all things. The best poetic images, while they resonate with possibilities for transformation, are resolutely concrete, specific, incarnational. Concepts such as *wonder,* or even *holiness,* are not talked about so much as presented for the reader's contemplation.

The Roman Catholic poet Anne Porter, for example, evokes the mystery of the incarnation, and the entire journey of Holy Week—the sweat and tears of Maundy Thursday and Good Friday, and the deep peace of Easter morning—in this look at an Easter lily,

> Whose whiteness
> is past belief
>
> Its blossoms
> The shape of trumpets
> are mute as swans
>
> But deep and strong as sweat
> Is their feral perfume.

The American Buddhist Margaret Gibson begins her poem "Making Salad" by speaking of an ordinary task:

> I rub the dark hollow of the bowl
> with garlic, near to the fire enough
> so that fire reflects on the wood,
> a reverie that holds emptiness
> in high regard.

The poet notices the hearth-fire reflected in the window above her sink and, opening the window, catches a glimpse of the Pleiades. Taking in the brisk autumn air, she writes:

> I watch the leaves swirl
> and part, gathering fresh light
> from Gemini, ten millennia away, fresh
> from Sirius—holding each burning leaf,

each jewel within whatever light
a speck of conscious mind can make,
unshadowed by reflection or design,

impartial. Out the tap, from a source
three hundred feet down, so close
I feel the shudder in the earth, water
spills over my hands, over the scallions
still bound in a bunch from the store.
I had thought to make salad, each element
cut to precision, tossed at random
in the turning bowl. Now I lay the knife
aside. I consider the scallions. I consider
the invisible field. Emptiness is bound
to bloom—the whole earth, a single flower.

Even if we do not make such glorious poems
out of our ordinary experiences, arranging Easter
lilies or making salad, we are free to contemplate
both emptiness and fullness, absence and presence in the everyday circumstances of our lives.
No less a saint than Thérèse of Lisieux admitted
in her *Story of a Soul* that Christ was most abun-
dantly present to her not "during my hours of
prayer...but rather in the midst of my *daily* occu-
pations" (emphasis mine). We can become aware
of and limit our participation in activities that do
not foster the freedom of thought that poetry and
religious devotion require; I cannot watch television, for example, and write a poem. I might be

inspired by something I hear or see on television, particularly in news interviews, but this is rare. The ordinary activities I find most compatible with contemplation are walking, baking bread and doing laundry.

My everyday experience of walking confirms the poet Donald Hall's theory that poetic meter originates in the bodily rhythm of arms and legs in motion. Walking certainly loosens up more than my leg muscles. The simple, repetitive movements also free my mind to brainstorm. I find bread baking to be a hands-on experience of transformation, and during the quiet times when dough is rising, I often sit and write, aiming for transformations of my own. As for laundry, I might characterize it as approaching the moral realm; there are days when it seems a miracle to be able to make dirty things clean. I once wrote an article on laundry, specifically the joys of hanging clothes on the line to dry, and sent it to the *New York Times Magazine*. I had thought I might get a warning about backsliding as a feminist, but was pleasantly surprised to hear from an editor that my essay had inspired everyone in the office to talk about their own laundry rituals, usually inherited from a mother or grandmother, but in one case from a father who had taught his children laundry as a military discipline; the son, now in his fifties, had admitted that he still starched and ironed his shirts the British Army way.

Laundry is universal—we all must do it, or figure out a way to get it done—and as I learned when writing my essay, it is also surprisingly particular. The editors decided to print my essay because they thought it might stir up in their readers the same sort of discussion that they had had in their office. I must have received a hundred letters, many with poignant childhood memories of hanging clothes out-of-doors, or of happily running through clotheslines full of fragrant, billowing sheets. My two favorite responses to the article came from an Israeli woman who told me that during the Gulf War, the government had warned people not to hang clothes out-of-doors, as a gas attack would pollute them. The mother of an infant, she had defied the warnings and hung her baby's clothes out-of-doors as a visible sign of hope. Another woman, an apparently stressed-out commuter with small children, wrote to say that to enjoy laundry at all I must have way too much time on my hands.

The often heard lament, "I have so little time," gives the lie to the delusion that the daily is of little significance. Everyone has exactly the same amount of time, the same twenty-four hours in which many a weary voice has uttered the gospel truth: "Sufficient unto the day is the evil thereof" (Mt 6:34, KJV). But most of us, most of the time, take for granted what is closest to us and is most universal. The daily round of sunrise and sunset, for example, that marks the coming and passing of each day, is no longer a symbol of human hopes, or of God's majesty, but a grind, something we must grit our teeth to endure. Our busy schedules, and even urban architecture, which all too often deprives us of a sense of the sky, has diminished our capacity to marvel with the psalmist in the passage of time as an expression of God's love for us and for all creation:

> It was God who made the great lights,
> *whose love endures forever;*
> the sun to rule in the day,
> *whose love endures forever;*
> the moon and stars in the night,
> *whose love endures forever.* (Ps 136: 7–9, GR)

When I think of the way that so many Americans live—so many long commutes on so many sterile highways, to jobs that all too often seem equally sterile—I stand in awe. To tell you the truth, I don't know how my sister does it. She is a divorced woman, a single mother, who supports two children. Every morning, she must get up, help her children prepare for school, prepare herself for work, drive the family across the Koolau Mountains of Oahu into Honolulu, and go to her job as an office manager—officially the "administrator"—of a high-powered law firm. The very thought of it would make me want to turn over and go back to sleep. Another day. Another dollar. And life is what happens to you when you are busy doing something else.

How does my sister manage, I wonder, let alone live her life with grace and wit and humor, and an occasional fiery blast of justified anger. (The managing partner of the law firm once reported to her that he had relished dismissing a self-important young attorney who had complained that my sister did not treat him with proper deference, by saying, "We did not hire her for her retiring personality.") Somehow, she keeps body and soul—and a law firm—together, and she provides a home and a measure of security for her children. Compared to many single mothers, she is fortunate. But the key to her life is not to be found in her job, the money, or the steady car and mortgage payments. It is instead the priestly charism of transformation. I have already presented an image of a priest as housewife; now I will play with its mirror image. As my sister has matured, accepting and growing into her responsibilities as a single mother, she has grown adept at recognizing and savoring the holy in the mundane circumstances of daily life. Finding spiritual refreshment in unlikely places, she can offer nourishment to her children.

She once told me, for example, that the daily commute has become invaluable to her as family time, a free-for-all in which she and the kids exchange stories, bad jokes and silly songs. It has become a time to take measure of her children, to learn how their day has gone (or allow them to articulate their anxious anticipation concerning how it might go) and above all, to reflect on their growing up. The children are in the process of becoming, being formed as human beings, and everything they do or say has the potential to inform their mother's decisions about how best to foster their growth, even a ferocious squabble over who gets to sit in the front seat, the "loser" sulking all the way home. No matter how dreary the weather, inside or outside the car, there are daily blessings to be found. She and the kids can count the new waterfalls that spring up on the cliffs through which they pass after a heavy rain. And, on the homeward trip, they have the astonishing view of the Pacific Ocean unfolding before them as they emerge from a tunnel in the mountains. It is a view that attracts tourists from all over the world. But the grip of acedia on the human spirit is such that even the great beauty of this land and seascape can be rendered impotent and invisible. It is common for people stationed in Hawaii with the military or large corporations to experience what is termed "rock fever," a condition marked by a nagging contempt for the place. They hate the ocean because it reminds them that they are stuck on an island in the middle of "nowhere," and they dismiss paradise as "the rock."

I am sure that my sister and her children often fail to notice the natural beauty that is laid before them, in splendid greens and blues. But sometimes just the sight of the sea can quell an argument, calming the atmosphere in the car. It can also stir things up, breaking through the family's insularity and the daily monotony of the commute. Being a parent is also daily, though hardly monotonous, and my sister has learned the spiritual discipline of so many parents, to help her children learn to build a family around the little events that make up the course of a day. A geographically distant but doting aunt, I am a grateful recipient of it all. I can easily picture my nine-year-old nephew offering a friend a "tour" of their house, starting not with his bedroom but with the bathroom, where he points to the toilet and says, "that's where I put all my troubles."

Like many children, my niece and nephew are budding theologians. When my nephew was eight, he chastised his mother for not intervening when a petty dispute escalated into hysteria. He said to his mother, "*You're* the grown-up—it's your responsibility. If you don't settle this, all hell will break loose!" Later, when he tried to smooth things over by asking his mom to play a game with him before bedtime, she rebuffed him. He threw his hands up into the air, and said, "Great! Now we'll go to bed angry with each other, and when we get up in the morning, we'll still be mad, and it

20

will never end!" She agreed to play the game. When I informed my nephew that what he had said was in the Bible, and that both Jesus and St. Paul would have given his mother similar advice, he responded with what for him is ultimate praise, a heartfelt, "Cool!"

Not long ago my eleven-year old niece reported to her mother that God speaks to her in her dreams. When my sister asked her how long this had been going on, she replied that it had begun when she was five. Among the more reassuring things that God has told her is that a little swearing is not the end of the world. God informed her that everyone is given a million opportunities to swear in a lifetime; it's only at a million and one that you are in danger of going to hell. To my niece, like any child, a million seems too many to count; she is reassured to think that even God can't possibly be bothered to keep track of the small stuff, the little "damns" uttered during a day. (Although she did tell God that she was worried about her little brother because she had heard him swear when he was only eight years old, and she thought if he kept it up he would use up his million chances in a hurry.)

The Bible is full of evidence that God's attention is indeed fixed on the little things. But this is not because God is a Great Cosmic Cop, eager to catch us in minor transgressions, but simply because God loves us—loves us so much that the divine

21

presence is revealed even in the meaningless workings of daily life. It is in the ordinary, the here-and-now, that God asks us to recognize that the creation is indeed refreshed like dew-laden grass that is "renewed in the morning" (Ps 90:5), or to put it in more personal and also theological terms, "our inner nature is being renewed every day" (2 Cor 4:16). Seen in this light, what strikes many modern readers as the ludicrous attention to detail in the book of Leviticus, involving God in the minutiae of daily life—all the cooking and cleaning of a people's domestic life—might be revisioned as the very love of God. A God who cares so much as to desire to be present to us in everything we do.

It is this God who speaks to us through the psalmist as he wakes from sleep, amazed, to declare, "I will bless you, Lord, you give me counsel, and even at night direct my heart" (Ps 16:7, GR). It is this God who speaks to us through the prophets, reminding us that by meeting the daily needs of the poor and vulnerable, characterized in the scriptures as the widows and orphans, we prepare the way of the Lord and make our own hearts ready for the day of salvation. When it comes to the nitty-gritty, what ties these threads of biblical narrative together into a revelation of God's love is that God has commanded us to refrain from grumbling about the dailiness of life. Instead we are meant to accept it gratefully, as a reality that humbles us even as it gives us cause for praise. The rhythm of sunrise and sunset marks a passage of time that makes each day rich with the possibility of salvation, a concept that is beautifully summed up in an ancient saying from the monastic tradition: "Abba Poemen said concerning Abba Pior that every day he made a new beginning."

According to Genesis, this is no more than God has asked of himself. Creation itself was a daily process—each day God spoke more and more into being, and then, it seems, let it all sit until the next day. Our bodies, and our lives, still reflect these basic rhythms of creation, which are also captured in the church's tradition of daily prayer, also known as the liturgy of the hours or the divine office. Lauds (or morning prayer) reminds us of our need to renew, to remember and recommit to this process of creation in our inmost selves. Those of you who are not "morning people" know how difficult this can be—and those of us who are subject to depression know that just getting up in the morning can be the greatest challenge of the day. The evening offices of vespers and compline, by comparison, are a surrendering of contention, a willingness to let the day go, and let God bring on the quiet, brooding darkness in which dreams might wrestle with and even nourish the soul. Each night, like the farmer of the gospel parable, we are asked to admit to the limitations of our conscious understanding, and enter into the realm of God: "The kingdom of

God is as if someone would scatter seed on the ground, and would sleep and rise night and day, and the seed would sprout and grow, he does not know how" (Mk 4:26–27).

Such worship, it seems to me, is *primary* theology, the fertile ground out of which our poems and stories, our theories and ideas—and even, to use a dauntingly sober word that I seldom employ except in jest, our hermeneutics—can grow. Remembering to praise God every morning, noon and evening establishes a primal rhythm, as primal as creation, and I know from experience how refreshing this can be in the life of a childless freelance writer whose days might otherwise have little rhythm or sacred routine. I insert the word *sacred* because I wrote my book *The Cloister Walk* in part to celebrate the grace that fell upon me when I was able to practice the daily liturgy—not only attending the eucharist but the complete liturgy of the hours—with a monastic community over many months. To my surprise, the monotonous, repetitive activity did not place a damper on my writing, but the opposite: the prose and poetry began to flow, in a near-constant stream. The wonder for me was that this was not at all a matter of wild, unfettered inspiration so much as a dialogue with the liturgy of the hours. It all depended on a steady, daily routine that by the standards of the busy world looked boring, repetitive, meaningless.

But when I am at home, without the scaffolding of daily communal prayer to sustain me, it is hard for me to sustain routine. I find the liturgy an especially hard discipline, one that I mostly fail at observing. I can easily identify with a comment made by Peter Jordan in a *Commonweal* article on Dorothy Day: "Lacking the formal monastic regimen, Day had to steal the early morning hours for her spiritual exercises. She did this almost daily, year in and year out." And I love the simple, unsanctimonious and humble thing that Day herself said about her practice: "My strength...returns to me with my cup of coffee and the reading of the psalms." Workaholism is the opposite of humility, and to an unhumble literary workaholic such as myself, morning devotions can feel useless, not nearly as important as getting about my business early in the day. I know from bitter experience that when I allow busy little doings to fill the precious time of early morning, when contemplation might flourish, I open the doors to the demon of acedia. Noon becomes a blur—no time, no time—the wolfing down of a sandwich as I listen to the morning's phone messages and plan the afternoon's errands. When evening comes, I am so exhausted that vespers has become impossible. It is as if I have taken the world's weight on my shoulders and am too greedy, and too foolish, to surrender it to God.

Having discarded contemplation, I render it, and the worship that is its fruit, meaningless, futile, without issue. And this dry sterility is the stuff of acedia. Like John Bunyan's pilgrim, having been captured by Giant Despair, I languish in the dungeon of Doubting Castle and need to be reminded that the key that would set me free is already in my possession. Worship has often proved to be that key; although on the surface it seems useless, it is also necessary, a means of reconnecting with other people when acedia or dejection has isolated me. Worship grounds me again in the real world of God's creation, dislodging me from whatever world I have imagined for myself. I have come to believe that when we despair of praise, when the wonder of creation and our place in it are lost to us, it's often because we've lost sight of our true role as creatures—we have tried to do too much, pretending to be in such control of things that we are indispensable. It's a hedge against mortality and, if you're like me, you take a kind of comfort in being busy. The danger is that we will come to feel too useful, so full of purpose and the necessity of fulfilling obligations that we lose sight of God's play with creation, and with ourselves.

Is it not a good joke that when God gave us work to do as punishment for our disobedience in Eden, it was work that can never be finished, but only repeated, day in and day out, season upon season, year after year? I see here not only God's keen sense of humor, but also a creative and zestful love. It is precisely these thankless, boring, repetitive tasks that are hardest for the workaholic or utilitarian mind to appreciate, and God knows that being rendered temporarily mindless as we toil is what allows us to approach the temple of holy leisure. When confronting a sinkful of dirty dishes—something I do regularly, as my husband is the cook in our house and I am the dishwasher—I admit that I generally lose sight of the fact that God is inviting me to play. But I recall that as a college student I sometimes worked as a teacher's aide in a kindergarten and was interested to note that one of the most popular play areas for both boys and girls was a sink in a corner of the room. After painting, the children washed their brushes there, but at other times, for the sheer joy of it— the tickle of water on the skin and God knows what else—a few children at a time would be allowed what the teacher termed "water play." The children delighted in filling, emptying and refilling plastic bowls, cups and glasses, watching bubbles form as they pressed objects deeper into the sink or tried to get others to stay afloat.

It is difficult for adults to be so at play with daily tasks in the world. What we do of necessity can drag us down, and all too often the repetitive and familiar become not occasions for renewal, but dry, stale, lifeless activity. When washing dishes, I am no better than anyone else at converting the drudgery of the work into something better by means of playful abandon. The contemplative in me recognizes the sacred potential in the mundane task, even as the terminally busy go-getter resents the necessity of repetition. But, as Søren Kierkegaard reminds us, "Repetition is reality, and it is the seriousness of life...repetition is the daily bread which satisfies with benediction." Repetition is both as ordinary and necessary as bread, and the very stuff of ecstasy. When reading a story such as *Peter Rabbit* to a small child, who among us has not heard that child summon the authority to say, "Read it again"? I once observed a girl of about four years of age find a penny on the floor of a post office. "Look, Momma, a penny," she said. Her mother, busy with the clerk at the window, mumbled an acknowledgement. I was surprised to see the girl put the penny back on the floor, in a different location. "Look, Momma," she said again, "I found another one!" She kept it up until she had found five pennies, and each one of them new.

The wisdom of that child is difficult for grown-ups to retain. At the very least, we are expected to keep such foolish little games to ourselves. Mystics and poets do get to play, but although much lip service is paid to both traditions in our culture, it is largely condescension. No parent really wants his or her child to grow up and become a poet; no one in a religious house really wants to live next door to a mystic. The task, and the joy, of writing for me is that I can play with the metaphors that God has placed in the world and present them to others in a way they will accept. My goal is to allow readers their own experience of whatever discovery I have made, so that it feels new to them, but also familiar, in that it is of a piece with their own experience. It is a form of serious play.

And it was in the play of writing a poem that I first became aware that the demands of laundry might have something to do with God's command that we worship, that we sing praise on a regular basis. Both laundry and worship are repetitive activities with a potential for tedium, and I hate to admit it, but laundry often seems like the more useful of the tasks. But both are the work that God has given us to do. The poem, which is printed below, is an attempt to convey one of the mysteries of housekeeping, the odd state I found myself in one day as I sought to make order out of the habitual chaos and clutter of my home. It had been a busy day, and I felt like a clown in a three-ring circus, taming the lion of my business correspondence, putting out the fake fires that seemed to spring up with each phone call and doing laundry that seemed endless, as in how many dirty clothes can fit inside the magic box of the washing machine.

Suddenly, I found myself at the foot of my basement stairs, and realized that I had little idea of what I was doing there and no memory of having descended the steps. My hands held clues, in the form of an item or two of dirty clothing, several books, an old dust pan and whisk broom, a box of crayons, and some thoroughly incongruous kitchenware—a coffee mug and a plastic pitcher with several matching tumblers. Operating in housewife mode, my brain had conceived of a place, the "right place," for all of these items in that basement, and I was about to set them there, in a finely tuned sequence of events that I had now forgotten. The experience struck me as comical. But I also recalled that when my husband had spent several weeks in a psychiatric ward, a woman there, an abused wife, had spoken of such an event as the precipitating cause of her hospitalization. She had been cleaning house in a frenzy so as to avoid the next beating, an attempt she knew to be futile. Then, all at once, she stopped, and stood frozen in her basement for well over an hour. She was in such dread of falling, of literally disappearing into nothingness within her house, that she had to crawl up the stairs and phone a neighbor who could telephone for medical assistance.

My dislocation, though a fleeting sort of madness, was far less drastic. But it made me ponder the nature of housecleaning, and that became the title of the poem. Rather than quote a few lines, I will print it in its entirety. I employ as an epigram a line from Nor Hall's book, *The Moon and the Vir-*

gin: "The dreamer descends through the base-ment to see what was valuable in her inheritance."

HOUSECLEANING

Kneeling in the dust, I recall
the church in Enna, Sicily,
where Ceres and Proserpine reigned
until a Pope kicked them out
in the mid-nineteenth century.

This is my Hades, where I find
what the house has eaten.
   And Jessica was left with only
   the raw, sheer, endless terror
   of being alone in the world.
"We are alone, Jessica," I say aloud;
the whole box of romances must go.

I keep the photograph of a young girl
reading cross-legged
under cottonwoods,
her belly still flat, not yet a fruit
split open, the child shining
in its membrane
like a pomegranate seed.

She ended both their lives,
and no mother's rage or weeping
could bring them back.
I leave her with the book of fairy tales:

still safe, held fast,
in Sleeping Beauty's bramble forest.

I could use some sleep.
What I do must be done
each day, in every season,
like liturgy. I pray
to Mary Magdalene, who kept seven
    demons,
one for each day of the week.
How practical; how womanly.

My barren black cat rubs against my legs.
I think of the barren women
exhorted by the Good Book
to break into song:
we should sing, dear cat,
for the children who will come in our old age.
The cat doesn't laugh,
but I do. She rolls in dust
as I finish sweeping.

I empty the washer
and gather what I need for the return:
the basket of wet clothes
and bag of clothes-pins,
a worn spring jacket in need of mending.
Then I head upstairs, singing an old hymn.

   I forget now where I picked up the detail about
the Sicilian church, a small tidbit in the venerable

history of the Christian church's encounter with ancient folk religion and myth. The lines from the cover of a romance novel come from a book I noticed as I was shelving it in a library where I once worked. A substantial portion of my family story is in the poem; condensed into a few lines is a fictionalized version of my Aunt Mary's suicide. She was an aunt on my father's side of the family, a woman who haunted me for years, ever since I learned when I was ten or eleven years old that she had killed herself in the year when I was born. Pregnant out of wedlock, she had been institutionalized for a mental illness that only seemed to worsen when the baby was born. There is evidence that Mary was schizophrenic, but I have long considered her suicide to be in part the result of both pre- and postpartum depression.

Another element in the poem concerns the move my husband and I made to my maternal grandmother's house in 1974. It was a house that she and my grandfather Totten had built in the early 1920s and lived in for over fifty years, but it always seemed more her house than his. My grandfather's true realm was his medical office on Main Street, but he also had the dark north bedroom of the house, where he took a nap every day after lunch—forbidden territory. From my child's perspective, the house seemed my grandmother's domain, where she made three square meals a day, every day, in the summers when we would visit. Where she worked laundry through a wringer washer in the basement and hung the wet clothes on a line in the backyard. I still use the Maytag washer that she purchased in the late 1960s. And I still hang clothes on the line—for the exercise, for the pleasing ozone aroma of clothes dried in sunlight, and sometimes, in winter, as a means of combating cabin fever.

During the unspeakably brutal winter of 1996–1997, with nearly thirty inches of snow on the ground by Thanksgiving, I had had enough by the time the spring blizzards came—another three feet of snow and high winds on the eighth of April—that I set out one morning, ablaze with the warmth of an angry determination, to shovel a path to the clothesline in order to hang something colorful there. As I began to handle the wet clothes, my hands quickly reddened, stung with cold, but it seemed worth doing nonetheless, simply to break the hold of winter on my spirit—and to disrupt the monotony of the white moonscape that our backyard had become. And even though the clothes freeze-dried stiffly and had to be thawed in the house, they had the sky-scent of summer on them. And it helped.

The poem, like housekeeping itself, is an attempt to bring order out of chaos. In the poem, by pulling many disparate things together, I tried to replicate the actual work of cleaning, sorting through the leftovers, the odd pieces of a life, in order to make a whole. I sense that striving for wholeness is, increasingly, a countercultural goal, as fragmented people make for better consumers, buying more bits and pieces—two or more cars, two homes and all that fills them—and outfitting one's body for a wide variety of identities: business person, homebody, amateur athlete, traveler, theater or sports fan. Things exercise a certain tyranny over us. Whenever I am checking bags at an airport, I recall St. Teresa of Avila's wonderful prayer of praise, "Thank God for the things that I do not own." Things are truly baggage, our impedimenta, which must be maintained with work that is menial, steady and recurring. But, like liturgy, the work of cleaning draws much of its meaning and value from repetition, from the fact that it is never completed, but only set aside until the next day. Both liturgy and what is euphemistically termed "domestic" work also have an intense relation with the present moment, a kind of faith in the present that fosters hope and makes life seem possible in the day-to-day.

My poem is in some sense "about" the mythic Proserpine (or Persephone), and I had great fun employing the elements of her story, the pomegranate seed that Hades induces her to eat so that she will have to keep returning to him, spending part of each year underground. Her story is, of course, the story of winter and spring, of the dying down of vegetation and its eventual rebirth. In an earlier poem, entitled "Persephone," I depicted her as a kind of pawn between the forces of death and life. Speaking of her own condition, she says:

> ...I learned to eat
> what was put before me,
> and became a wife.
>
> My mother raged, my husband
> capitulated. When the deal was struck
> no one thought I'd be torn in two.
>
> Now I have my pied-à-terre,
> and the inner darkness.
> Now spring is a blind green wall.

Spring can seem to me like "a blind green wall," an implacable force stirring things into life that has grown comfortably dormant. It is one of the perversities of my interior makeup that I so often become depressed just as winter makes its turn into spring, and the longed-for moment arrives; the weather turns pleasant, and one can walk out of doors without bundling up. But unbundling means exposure, a kind of vulnerability, and I seldom feel ready for it when that first balmy day arrives. Instead, I resist the good news of spring, lurking inside my house as if it is still winter. My spirit suffers, my garden languishes, and my perennial flowers and herbs must struggle on their own with encroaching weeds. This bleak mood always passes, but in the meantime I am like the person spoken of in Sirach 27:30: "Anger and wrath...are abominations, yet the sinner holds on to them." Choosing interior darkness, I draw the house around me like a shroud and protect my despair.

I am always distressed to find how fearfully I confront the glorious prospect of spring and summer, their tantalizing invitation to the out-of-doors and ease of movement. In my sour mood I become like the Israelites in the desert who rage against the God who has freed them. Their servitude in Egypt, as oppressive as it was, had also offered a kind of security. But the people grow terrified by the prospect of freedom, the unknown way that lies before them, and their bitterness is profound. They say to Moses, as Pharaoh's army closes in on them, "Is it because there were no graves in Egypt that you have taken us away to die in the wilderness? What have you done to us, bringing us out of Egypt?...it would be better for us to serve the Egyptians than to die in the wilderness" (Ex 14:11). Three times they raise up this lament: at the Red Sea, in the desert when they are hungry and can find no food and when they and their livestock are exhausted with thirst at their camp at Rephidim. Each time Moses pleads with God, and each time God answers with a miracle. The parting of the sea, the gift of manna, the water from the rock. After he has drawn water, at God's command, from the rock at

Horeb, Moses names the springs after Hebrew verbs meaning "to test" and "to find fault." Marking the lack of steadfastness that seems to be an integral part of the human psyche, Moses immortalizes Israel's doubt, "[calling] the place Massah and Meribah, because the Israelites quarreled and tested the Lord, saying, 'Is the Lord among us or not?'" (Ex 17:7).

When I was a child, these stories of Israel in the desert were my favorite in the Bible. Of course I always sided with God, wondering how in the world these foolish people could fail to trust time and time again, after all that God had done for them. Now that I am older, I know all too well and can easily see myself among the doubters and complainers. Even when I was young, however, I had some appreciation of the repetitions as a narrative device. They allowed me a form of play in which I could respond to each story by raising my own lament: *not again!* Are they going to test God yet again? And every spring, as I contend with depression, I must ask this question of myself: again? When will you ever learn? even though the answer seems to be never. Just as Adam and Eve left Eden in order to take on work that is never finished but must be repeated, so there are spiritual matters that I must contend with over and over again, whenever I am confronted with the genuinely new, even the expected newness of spring.

Winter has become a comfortable place to wallow in gloom, my Egypt, the devil I know; but I must cast it off in order to welcome the burgeoning green life out-of-doors. And often it is the necessity of doing laundry that provides the way. No matter how lethargic I am feeling—and an overwhelming listlessness is a sure sign of acedia—I find it morally reprehensible to use an automatic clothes dryer when I could hang clothes out-of-doors to dry. So I literally emerge from my basement carrying a clothes basket and I leave the cave of winter behind. Once I am out-of-doors, of course, I must take stock of the garden to see what needs to be done there. Even if it takes me a few more days to muster the energy to do the work, I have put the greening garden within my range of vision and within my psyche. I am always glad to see the columbines return; most of them were planted by my grandmother many years ago. Even if all of this fails to cheer me, at the very least, by the end of the day my husband and I have clean, fragrant clothes, towels and sheets.

Although I did not realize it until many years after I wrote "Housecleaning," the poem is a manifesto against acedia. In her terrifying autobiographical novel *The Bell Jar* Sylvia Plath has her protagonist, Esther, explain why she has not washed her hair for three weeks: "The reason I hadn't washed my clothes or my hair was because it seemed so silly....It seemed so silly to wash one day when I would have to wash again the next. It made me tired just to think of it. I wanted to do everything at once and for all and be through with it." Here, as clear as the tolling of a bell, is the awful death wish of our ancient foe, acedia, a perfect expression of the deep-seated, ironic contempt for the self that has become all too fashionable in our day. Esther's lack of concern for her body is not the healthy, ascetic humility of a desert amma but the dread of a young woman who is rapidly becoming psychotic.

Our culture's ideal self, especially the accomplished, professional self, rises above necessity, the humble, everyday, ordinary tasks that are best left to unskilled labor. The comfortable lies we tell ourselves regarding these "little things"—that they don't matter, and that daily personal and household chores are of no significance to us spiritually—are exposed as falsehoods when we consider that reluctance to care for the body is one of the first symptoms of extreme melancholia. Shampooing the hair, washing the body, brushing the teeth, drinking enough water, taking a daily vitamin, going for a walk, as simple as they seem, are acts of self-respect. They enhance one's ability to take pleasure in oneself and in the world. At its Greek root the word *acedia* means "lack of care," and indifference to one's welfare can escalate to overt acts of self-destruction and even suicide. Care is not passive—the word derives from an

Indo-European word meaning "to cry out," as in a lament. Care asserts that as difficult and painful as life can be, it is worth something to be in the present, alive, doing one's daily bit. It addresses and acts on the daily needs that acedia would have us suppress and deny.

Caring is one response to the grief of the human condition, a condition described so poignantly in Psalm 90: "Our span is seventy years,/or eighty for those who are strong./And most of these are emptiness and pain./They pass swiftly and we are gone" (Ps 90:10, GR). But lack of care is another response, and it takes many forms, from suicidal depression to a madcap superficiality, to the practiced pretending-to-indifference at which adolescents excel. When I read Esther's confident words, which seem intended to mask her well-reasoned insanity (what a psychiatrist might identify as a "well-detended neurosis"), I recall my brash and bratty fourteen-year-old self responding to my mother's suggestion that I make my bed in the morning before leaving for school. "Why?" I asked, in a mocking tone. "Why? I'll just have to undo it again at night." My mother had no answer that would have satisfied me then, and I complied with her request in as perfunctory a manner as possible. It was nothing, just a small expression of ordinary sloth. I was slow to recognize that combating sloth, being willing to care for oneself and others on a daily basis, is no small part of what constitutes basic

41

human sanity, a faith in the everyday. Not until I was in my thirties did I discover Benedict's Rule for monasteries, in which he characterizes sloth as disobedience.

I have long been intrigued by the questions Jesus asks his disciples in the gospel of Mark—"Who do you say that I am?" (Mk 9:29), and "What is it you want me to do for you?" (10:36). By extension, as we too are Christ's disciples, he is directing these questions to us as well. For me, the latter usually occasions a despairing sigh—"Lord, there is so much that I would ask of you"—but then I recall the passage in the letter to the Hebrews in which we are reminded that Christ has already done everything for us. It speaks of the Christ who "offered for all time a single sacrifice for sins" (Heb 10:12). And yet the church teaches, and our experience of faith confirms, that Christ continues to be with us and to pray for us. The paradox may be unraveled, I think, if we remember that when human beings try to "do everything at once and for all and be through with it," we court acedia, self-destruction and death. Such power is reserved for God, who alone can turn what is "already done" into something that is ongoing and ever present. It is a quotidian mystery.

Modern psychology does not always know what to make of mystery, but it is in agreement with the psychology of the ancient desert monastics in recognizing that depression is often the flip side of anger. What we perceive as dejection over the futility of life is sometimes greed, which the monastic tradition perceives as rooted in a fear of being vulnerable in a future old age, so that one hoards possessions in the present. But most often our depression is unexpressed anger, and it manifests itself as the sloth of disobedience, a refusal to keep up the daily practices that would keep us in good relationship to God and to each other. For when people allow anger to build up inside, they begin to perform daily tasks resentfully, focusing on others as the source of their troubles. Instead of looking inward to find the true reason for their sadness—with me, it is usually a fear of losing an illusory control—they direct it outward, barreling through the world, impatient and even brutal with those they encounter, especially those who are closest to them. I recognize all of these stages in myself and I know that there are some days when unspecific anger makes me of little use to anyone. The popular faith in "talking it out" is counterproductive; if I bristle with irritability, especially if my anger seems out of proportion to any cause, depression is my real enemy. And talking about it is the last thing I need to do. It either leads me to rant, or it allows self-pity to surface, sending the poison deeper within.

When, in the early 1980s, I discovered in the sayings of the desert abbas and ammas a name for the state of despondency that had troubled me since adolescence, I also learned that its remedy was to be found in what the monks called "the gift of tears." I found it paradoxical but also refreshing to consider that only by embracing grief and refusing to run from it could salvation from despair be found. As Amma Syncletica said,

> There is grief that is useful, and there is grief that is destructive. The first sort consists in weeping over one's own faults and weeping over the weakness of one's neighbors, in order not to destroy one's purpose, and attach oneself to the perfect good. But there is also a grief that comes from the enemy, full of mockery, which some call *accidie*. This spirit must be cast out, mainly by prayer and psalmody.

That we suffer from spiritual ailments the desert Christians knew very well. And they knew the value of spiritual remedy. But our modern mindset, with its faith in therapy, has been slow to recognize the value of that earlier wisdom. At its root the word *therapy* means "to hold up, to support." It gives us a sense that we are doing something, attending to our problems or those of other people. Like Diogenes of Corinth, who is said to have rolled up and down the streets in a cask so as not to be seen doing nothing when the barbarians stormed the gates of the city, when trouble strikes we roll out the support groups and counseling sessions and hope that it does some good. And often it does. But the never-ending work of therapy unfortunately can feed both our sense of self-importance and our fear of futility. People in therapy are encouraged to say that they are perpetually "in recovery," but not that they are cured.

The word *healing,* however, comes from a word meaning "entire," "complete." At the very least, it designates a change of condition, a conversion, a restoration to wholeness. For that reason it strikes me as a more religious word than therapy.

Perhaps the most radical thing about the psychology of the desert monastics, the hardest for us to grasp, is the extent to which they believed, as Amma Syncletica's statement reveals, that scripture itself had the power to heal. And while it seems like an anachronism to agree with them, deep down I am certain that they are right. There are needs that cannot be met by our therapeutic methods but are amenable to the healing power of the word of God. There are people like myself, who have benefited from counseling on occasion, but are better served in the long run by more spiritual methods, and by such religious practices as "prayer and psalmody."

We all have demons, although we're usually more comfortable these days referring to them as "problems," "dysfunctions" or "issues." And exorcising them may still be one of the functions of scripture, employing "prayer and psalmody," as Amma Syncletica put it, to send the demons packing. It is true that they generally will return, but we will be stronger people then, more ready for the fight. (And prayer, as one desert monk put it, is warfare to the last breath.) I was late to discover the healing properties of scripture to which Amma Syncletica refers, and even now, when I am in the grip of acedia, my listlessness can prevent me from reaching for the words that I know would help—the Lord's Prayer or the lectionary readings for the day. When this occurs I have learned to scale down my expectations.

The late poet William Stafford, with his typical humble wit, used to say that he never suffered from "writer's block" because when he found himself unable to write, he simply lowered his standards. In a similar way, having recognized that when it comes to prayer, perfectionism is a born ally to acedia, I agree to lower my standards, dying down to the roots, as it were. And I rely on simple ejaculatory prayers, hymns and bits of the psalms that I know by heart. One of the best prayers I know is the quick, potent exclamation that John Cassian recommends as the basic prayer of the monk, and that Benedictines still use to open their liturgies: "O God, make haste to my rescue,/Lord come to my aid!" (Ps 70:2, GR). And there is the Hail Mary and the basic "Jesus prayer" of the monastic and Orthodox traditions: "Lord, Jesus Christ, have mercy on me, a sinner."

In reclaiming my Christian faith, I have learned that such simple prayers, uttered at odd moments during the day, are an integral part of my process of conversion. And having to ask God for help also reminds me that I need the help of other people, as no one makes this journey alone. When I was beginning to find my way back to church after some twenty years away, I was remarkably dependent on the help of others, which was not a comfortable experience for someone who had grown accustomed to the independence of a freelance writer. "Housecleaning" is one of many poems that I wrote in the mid-1980s, during my first encounters with a spiritual director. I could not have used the term back then, for I did not know it. To me he was simply a pastor whose friendship and mentoring I desperately needed if I was to make the transition that had come to seem so important to me. But it was also a scary time, and the change I sought seemed impossible. Church services were both emotionally engaging and yet remote, so much so that I did not have much hope that I would ever feel as if I belonged there.

In those early days of my conversion, the writing of poems became the primary indicator of my "pilgrim's progress." What emerged out of my unconscious as lines of verse became the raw material that the pastor worked with in guiding me on my journey. And this is one of the poems in which I made a kind of quantum leap; in it my burgeoning but as yet unformed religious faith surfaced with a confidence I could not yet claim for myself on a conscious level. I realized, even as I was writing it, that the poem was about much more than house-cleaning. The line, "What I do must be done/each day, in every season,/like liturgy," has proved prophetic for me. I have since spent many hours at prayer with the Benedictines, learning from them about liturgy as a kind of caring that not only encompasses the daily rituals of spiritual house-keeping, but extends into the communion of saints as worship, a communal expression of the praise that is God's due.

But when I wrote the line, I still had little sense of what liturgy was, or that it was indeed a daily venture. I had only recently become aware of the Benedictine monasteries in western North Dakota that were to play so important a part in helping me rediscover my religious faith. And as those lines about liturgy sprang up from deep within, I sensed that they were important, but had little idea of why this should be. I recalled the wisdom of my first writing teacher, Ben Belitt, who said, "Our poems are wiser than we are." No small part of the process of writing is the lifting up into consciousness of what has long remained in the basement, hidden, underground, as in a tomb.

Glancing again at the poem, I wonder if Mary

Magdalene is not only the first apostle, so named by no less a biblical authority than St. Jerome, but the church's first mystic as well. In John's gospel, she is the first to encounter the risen Christ, the first he calls by name after his resurrection. My Greek icon of the scene, a postcard given to me by a friend, has a passage on the back from a homily of Gregory the Great in which he invokes the Song of Songs: "If she was the only one to see him then," Gregory writes, "it is because she had persevered in seeking him. For perseverance lends strength to every good action. Thinking of the same Spouse, the Church, his Bride, sings: 'On my bed I sought him who is the beloved of my soul.' "

It has become risky to use bridal imagery in religious circles, especially feminist ones. These days, calling a nun or a sister "a bride of Christ" might earn you a kick in the shins. But we would be foolish indeed to excise the image from our religious treasury merely because it has been so egregiously misused in the past. (I must say that when it comes to evincing an abiding respect for poetry, the Roman Catholic tradition has it all over the Protestant one, despite the fact that for at least a hundred years the Vatican has demonstrated a remarkable ability to literalize religious metaphors within an inch of their lives.) But when gently employed, used with respect both for women and the complex, mysterious nature of metaphor itself, the bride remains a lively, vivid image—we can see her, and feel the radiance of her smile—and thus she conveys, far better than the vague abstractions of psychobabble ever could, the pursuit Jesus makes of each one of us. This is the lover of our souls, as foretold by the prophet Isaiah:.

> You shall no longer be termed Forsaken,
> and your land shall no more be termed
>   Desolate
> but you shall be called My Delight is in Her,
> and your land Married,
> and your land shall be married.
> For as a young man marries a young woman,
> so shall your builder marry you,
> and as the bridegroom rejoices over the
>   bride,
> so shall your God rejoice in you. (Is 62:4–5)

Why not call ourselves, men and women, "lovers of Christ"? Not only priests or religious, but *all* Christians, lovers, intimates who trust in Christ to pray for us, and to know us fully, in our weaknesses and strengths. All Christians, faithful spouses, who know that Christ is present with us in our lives, "for better for worse, for richer for poorer, in sickness and in health," whatever befalls. It sounds so good, so godly; the high romance of First Corinthians, chapter 13.

In that famous "love chapter," St. Paul is speaking not of romantic love, but of the love that endures long after the initial ardor of courtship has cooled. For just as lovers become brides, brides become spouses, and that is where the specter of the daily appears. Like the jealous fairy at Sleeping Beauty's christening, it slips into the hearts of wedding guests and scatters a tinge of doubt, a nagging fear that the intimate relationship being celebrated will not stand the test of time, which is to say that it will founder in the day-to-day. "Do you want to know how serious our fight was?" a friend said to me, when once I happened upon her and her husband of thirty years at a tense moment. Her voice rising, brittle with rage, she said, "It was over the little garbage can in the bathroom." "That bad," I said, asking if they needed an exorcist—not that I was offering my services. The husband's laugh was a half sigh, and he said, wearily, "Just about."

Thirty years of marriage imply a certain stability, but quarrels over trivial household matters remind us that human relationships cannot be taken for granted. In contemplating marriage, or any long-term commitment to others as a quotidian mystery, it might help to regard the gifts of our hearts as being like the manna God sent each day to the Israelites in their journey through a forbidding wilderness. God has made us so that abundant grace can flow from us in response to great need, but in order to fulfill its

God-given purpose, such grace must be received and used up, as it is of the present moment and will not keep even overnight. But acedia seeks to hoard against the time when God is no longer present, and we can't trust the nourishment that other people offer. It rejects the present moment in favor of a vainglorious and imaginary future in which we will do just fine, thank you, at providing for ourselves. And this is an attitude that can break the deep covenant that holds a marriage together. In contemplating the "daily bread" that we ask for in the Lord's Prayer, Simone Weil asserts that God has created us so that the present is all we have. "The effective part of [our] will," Weil writes, "is not effort, which is directed toward the future. It is consent; it is the 'yes' of marriage. A 'yes' pronounced within the present moment and for the present moment, but spoken as an eternal word, for it is consent to the union of Christ with the eternal part of our soul."

This is all well and good—I believe it is very good—but with that last remark, as Weil drop kicks us into the Trinity (perhaps thinking of John 15's "You will know that I am in my Father, and you in me, and I in you") she also employs the sort of richly textured religious language that can lead us astray. Weil's statement is not only beautiful but true. However, I would caution that language such as this, lovely and resonant as it is, can cushion the radical nature of our intimacy with God and make Christian discipleship sound far too easy. What seems terribly spiritual, holy and mysterious can lull us into an unholy complacency, and lead us away from probing the areas of our lives that need the most attention if we are to be faithful to God and to each other. I suspect that Weil, a tough-minded thinker, would agree that such religious language requires us to be vigilant and to guard against spiritual vainglory, against anything that would allow us to disincarnate our faith and escape into the ether of gnosticism. In seeking any covenantal relationship we must be willing to say "yes" long before we have a clear idea of what such intimacy will cost us. Marriage is eternal, but it's also daily, as daily and unromantic as housekeeping. And in marriage, as in the monk's cell, acedia finds a good hunting ground.

Most brides eventually become mothers, and I employ the word *barren* in my poem advisedly, knowing that, for many women, it carries a good deal of religious and psychological baggage. I use it because it allows me to refer to Sarah's laughter—heartfelt, I imagine—at hearing that God intends for her to bear a child when she is long past menopause. And it allows me to allude to Isaiah's "Sing, O barren one; burst into song and shout, you who have not been in labor!" (Is 54:1). But there is no getting around the fact that in the history of human culture, including that of

53

ancient Israel, a woman's failure to conceive a child has often been considered a curse. And in our own society, while being childless is no longer interpreted as a sign of God's disfavor, many infertile couples seem to feel cursed. Some are so desperate to conceive that they spend many thousands of dollars at fertility clinics. As for myself, having never fulfilled the biological purpose—some would say woman's primary purpose—of conceiving and bearing a child, I have rendered myself useless by the standards of the world. I do not know if I am infertile for any physical reason, as I have never pursued the question. This is because when I was about fifteen years of age, I realized that I was not cut out to be a mother.

I can't explain this; it was not a choice, but a kind of deep knowing, a radical understanding of my situation and my self that came with the sort of bedrock certainty that I have come to associate with the mystical tradition. But as a Protestant girl who was only dimly aware of Roman Catholic religious orders or the Christian mystics, I did not have the language to conceive of this sudden knowledge in religious terms, as a vow. I made no promise, no conscious decision. All that happened was that I was suddenly confronted by an inner voice, one that I had not heard before, telling me that motherhood was not advisable for me. I accepted this, perhaps too readily, as I was terrified by the notion of pregnancy; the physical upheaval, the bodily and psychic vulnerability, the blood and pain of labor. Frankly—and here I have to laugh at my timorous adolescent self—at a time when the rare occasion of a boy telephoning me was enough to scare me out of my wits, sex and its cumbersome apparatus (dating, kissing, necking, going steady and all the rest, subjects of intense but woefully ignorant speculation among my friends at school) did not seem worth the trouble. Boys and babies were nice enough in their place, but too much for me to consider at the time. Homework seemed more pressing, and reading was much safer than navigating the social world of my peers. I knew that I was immature, but had the strong sense that I simply needed more time to grow up, to work through what would be required of me as an adult.

There was no one in my life to suggest that, at the bottom of all of this, if I could sort through the fears and be certain that I was not merely attempting to avoid coming to terms with my human sexuality, I might be nurturing the seeds of a religious vocation, an orientation toward a contemplative love that might be expressed in ways other than in genital intimacy, marriage and procreation. The religion I was exposed to around that time did not seem capable of being so intimately concerned with such things; it was a highly politicized, intellectual, liberal Protestant Christianity that put much more stock in ideas than in the questions that had begun to consume me. I received from it a strong dose of the historical critical method, and a demythologizing of scripture, whose main effect was to convince me that there was little anymore in religion for me. For spiritual solace I began to look to poetry.

And at college, homesick for my family and feeling an intense dislocation at having moved from Hawaii to Vermont, I withdrew into reading and writing, allowing a very few friendships to penetrate my inner defenses. People who have come to know me in recent years find this hard to believe, but I was so shy that I sometimes went for days without speaking a single word unless someone made a sustained attempt to draw me out. My scholarship job at the library provided me with one of my few social outlets outside of class. At the time I would not have thought to say so, but I had become a bit nunnish—quiet, withdrawn and obviously virginal—and this made for high comedy at Bennington College in the 1960s, a place where there were very few rules regarding students' behavior—no curfews, and only a cursory check in the morning by another student to make sure that we were alive and reasonably awake in our beds. If a boyfriend had spent the night in the dorm or if a girl had stayed in a nearby motel prostituting herself with truck drivers or Dartmouth students, as some of my friends did in this heady era of "sex, drugs and rock and roll," other students, and the institution itself, tended to look the other way.

Somehow, in this wild, anything-goes environment, I managed to create a cloister for myself, although I did not know the word except as a term of architectural history. All I knew of monasticism was that it had left behind splendid medieval churches (and many ruins) throughout Europe. My "monasticism" was an internal and existential one, and my dormitory room became a kind of a recluse's cell, a place where I escaped into books and, increasingly, into writing. It was also a place where people sometimes came when they were having a bad LSD trip, crashing from a brittle methamphetamine "high," or hiding out from an abusive boyfriend. In hindsight, although I was every bit as young, confused and misguided as my classmates, there was some holiness in this, and some pastoral dimension to the hospitality I was able to provide.

During my senior year, my peculiar role was formally recognized when, at one of the Sunday night socials in my dorm, we were inspired to invent titles for all the residents; I was designated as the "Pope." I protested; I had wanted to be the "Poet." (We already had an Oracle, a Scribe, a Painter, Terpsichore and a Knight Errant, the perfect title for the gallant Peter-Pan-like lesbian who was my neighbor.) But the group stood firm, and I had to serve as Pope for an entire school year. My vestment for official occasions—on Sunday evenings, and at a few other parties held in our dorm—was a *holoku,* an elegant type of muumuu that had once been reserved for Hawaiian royalty. Someone suggested that if I were Pope I would need a text to preach from; we chose *Alice in Wonderland.* And this is what passed for liturgy at Bennington College in the 1960s, when our having a college chaplain, or any campus ministry program, would have been inconceivable. Our only religions were the unofficial ones of art and psychiatry. Perhaps it is not surprising to find that, as silly as the schoolgirl nicknames and Sunday night rituals were, they did provide the young women of my dorm with a small measure of communal identity.

The fact that I had remained a virgin well into my senior year seemed almost to alarm many of my friends; I know it astonished the school doctor. While I accepted jokes about my being "the Virgin of Bennington," or "Norris the Nun," there was no true religious dimension to my situation. Nor was it a matter of ethics. While my way of being was clearly other, vastly different from that of so many of my classmates, it was primarily a means of escaping from other people and the demands of adulthood, rather than the self-giving that a true religious vocation requires. As yet, I had not enough self to give; I was still a human being in formation, trying to survive in an environment that I often found harsh, disorienting, bewildering.

My quintessential Bennington experience, one that replicated itself many times and in myriad forms during my four years there, occurred during my very first class, a freshman literature course. Used to the dress and conduct codes of a strict preparatory school, I was pleasantly surprised to find girls sprawled in the living room of one of the dorms, sitting on the floor, in window-seats and on sofas. I found a chair, and another girl in jeans—that was our uniform—took a space on the floor nearby. I was relieved to find that I liked the class, but I found this girl distracting, since all during class she chain-smoked, drank bottles of Coca-Cola and every now and then would take a little white pill. Finally, when class had ended, I asked her how she was feeling. When she gave me a blank stare, I couldn't resist saying that I didn't think it was a good idea to take so much aspirin. She looked at me as if I were the stupidest person she had ever encountered and snarled, "This isn't aspirin; it's speed." And I became Alice, flying down the rabbit hole, having no idea where I was, or what strange universe I had landed in. I barely knew what "speed" was, and the thought that someone my age would be addicted to it had never before crossed my mind.

Remaining underground as it were, withdrawing inwardly, even as I cautiously explored the terrain into which I had stumbled, was possibly the only sensible response I could have made. By the spring of my senior year I had gained some perspective on my life at Bennington. Grateful for much that I had found there, notably the encouragement I received as a writer, I was able to characterize my years at the college as a time of incubation, a protective brooding that had indeed prepared me to break out of my shell. But in many ways the college had been a difficult place for me, so steeped in the culture of the urban East that, as a Westerner, I never felt quite at home there.

One of my few constants, besides a love of literature, art and music that had been well nourished at Bennington, was the internal conviction I had carried with me since high school, that whatever I was destined for, it was not motherhood. This was a deep-rooted certainty in me long before I encountered the word *feminism* late in my college career. My inner certitude remained indifferent to ideology. And it was not something I could readily understand. I did wonder why, as I had excellent models for mothering in my own mother and maternal grandmother, I was so convinced that I was unsuited for it. My paternal grandmother and my Aunt Mary had provided a model of motherhood that was much more strained and conflicted; my grandmother had seen marriage to a Methodist pastor and childrearing as her form of ministry to the church, and it must have often seemed a thankless task. She had been determined that her sons would become ministers, but neither did. And her sister, a medical missionary in the Congo, used every opportunity to belittle her having settled for being "just" a wife and mother. As for my Aunt Mary, she had demonstrated an incapacity for motherhood that proved fatal, and I no doubt wondered if becoming a mother would be too great a strain on my own psyche. But mostly, my leaning toward childlessness seemed inexplicable, a matter of self-knowledge so interior that it was many years before I could express it in words.

Other convictions that had seemed so strong in early adolescence fell by the way: that by some magic I would become a great flutist, an Olympic swimmer, an inventor who would devote my great fortune to philanthropy. That I would never marry or ever become sexually intimate with a man. (I was unpopular enough with boys in high school that for a time this had seemed a foregone conclusion.) But, with one notable exception, whenever I would probe my psyche for the answer to the question—should I set my sights on motherhood—the answer was always no.

Only once, at a particularly vulnerable time when I was in my early twenties, did I fantasize at length about having a baby. Predictably enough, the temptation came as a love affair was coming to

61

a bad end. Just when I should have been glad to become free of an inappropriate and unhealthy relationship—the man was married, much older than myself, and, as I had discovered, a habitual philanderer—I was astonished to find myself strongly attracted, both physically and psychically, to the profoundly idiotic idea that having a baby would be a way for me to cling to the initial joy that I had found in the romance. I now know many other women who have had a similar experience, but at the time I was both enthralled and terrified by what seemed like a unique desire to have a child. Fortunately I was quick to recognize the dreadful fallacy in my wishful thinking—all too often, I suspect, insecure young women allow themselves to become pregnant using just such pathetic reasoning.

This was, as you might imagine, a barren time in my life, when I could mistake such a sordid love affair for the real thing. I had been attracted by the romantic "highs"—thinking that I was in love with this man and anticipating our dates with great longing—but I was quickly disillusioned. I had to learn the hard way that the "lows" of an adulterous affair are low indeed, and romance is not love. A short-lived fascination with another person may be exciting—I think we've all seen people aglow, in a state of being "in love with love"—but such an attraction is not sustainable over the long run. Paradoxically, human love is sanctified not in the height of attraction and enthusiasm but in the everyday struggles of living with another person. It is not in romance but in routine that the possibilities for transformation are made manifest. And that requires commitment.

"It is the nature of God to make the barren fertile...to have mercy on those who languish in hopelessness," writes Donald Witherup, in the *Collegeville Pastoral Dictionary of Biblical Theology.* And this early relationship did teach me much about what I did not want in life, namely, to ever again engage in the cruel, demeaning and exhausting subterfuges of adultery. And in the roundabout, backward way by which my learning so often proceeds, it also helped me to learn to love the right way. This seems awful to admit, but even as I had been seduced by an older man, I had been all too willing to enter into a relationship in which there was no possibility of commitment. I had been testing the waters of adult relationship, and now, having experienced what a lack of commitment and trust could do, I was determined to seek something better. And God's mercy and inexhaustible fertility are such that much good came from what might have been an irredeemable mess. The man's wife began to weary of his infidelities, and not long after he had dumped me for yet another college student, she divorced him. As for me, it was the illusion of love that had drawn me to New York City; I very much doubt that I would otherwise have had the nerve to set out for the big city on my own. And my job there, in arts administration, had introduced me to the notion of writing as a true vocation and taught me that it was possible for a writer to live by her wits. This, in turn, is what gave me the nerve to move to South Dakota and try my hand as a freelance writer.

My story is not in the least extraordinary; it is one among many stories I might have told about a young American woman coming of age in the late twentieth century. But it is the story I have lived day-to-day. Yet it also seems—and this is ordinary too—a story of transformation so profound that I wonder if I would now recognize the person I was at eighteen, or twenty-two. When I was a novice poet, just a few years out of college, I confided to an older and more experienced writer that one of the reasons I felt compelled to move from New York City to South Dakota was that the Plains were where my roots were. Surprising, and even scaring myself, as I had not before articulated this to anyone, and had not even been conscious of this desire in myself, I said that I thought there may be a book for me out on the Plains. "Why?" the other writer asked, in a dubious tone of voice. Reduced to mumbling, I replied, "Well, maybe I'd write about my family out there." "Why?" he said again, "What's so special about your family?"

I wish I could report that he had said this in a

teacherly manner, gently challenging me to serious reflection and response. But his words were dismissive and scornful in tone; they seemed designed to shut me up. I had learned not to be surprised at gratuitous cruelty among the writers that I met in the intensely competitive literary world of New York City, but this broke my stride. And it did shut me up, at least for a time. It was not uncommon, in the early 1970s, for up-and-coming male writers to treat young women writers with the contempt that I experienced that day. How dare you presume that you, of all people, even have a story, let alone think that you are fit to write it! But, looking back at the person I was then, I realize that I had not given this man much hope that I might amount to much, either as a writer or a human being. I was naive, immature, flighty, ungrounded. I was adrift, having made a sort of secret pact with myself to refuse to be really present in my own life. I often felt invisible then, as if I could slip through life without having an effect on other people. Given the curious Sleeping Beauty mentality that I exhibited at the time, I am sure that I did not yet take myself seriously as a writer, and it no longer surprises me that another writer would not have taken me seriously. I suspect that he had written me off as a foolish girl, just the sort to write poetry in the protective environment of college, but who would stop once the pressures of making a living took hold.

A grace is something that merits gratitude. The word *gratuitous* comes from the same root. The story that I was to write remained underground, gestating, for nearly twenty years, and I am ready to claim this as a grace. As was that other writer's cruel question, which eventually proved a useful one. As I began writing *Dakota,* my first book of personal narrative, it nagged at me, and I had to ask myself: What is so special about my family, this story? I realized that if I were to tell it I would have to labor to make it meaningful to others. It is a story that I have now been telling in prose over the past five years, the story of a faith unfolding out of a family, out of a life. It is not special, but absolutely ordinary. And that, too, is grace.

The late poet Paul Zweig once wrote, "If there is an Eden, it is not past, but coming," and this gives me the confidence to say that as adults, particularly adult women, we might best confront the mystery of our daily lives by doing as Jesus suggests, and look to small children, who have a wondrous capacity for living in the present moment with an innocent hope in what they learn to call the future. When my niece Christina was a toddler—she is now twenty—her mother worked as a stockbroker and financial planner. My brother, Christina's father, who is a Disciples of Christ pastor, would drive her to day care in the morning, and her mother would pick her up after work. And every afternoon she brought Christina an orange, peeled so that the child could eat it on the way home. One day Christina was busying herself by playing "Mommy's office" on the front porch of our house in Honolulu, and I asked her what her mother did at work. Without hesitation, and with a conviction that I relish to this day, she looked up at me and said, "She makes oranges."

And that is what God does, I think, making oranges and wind and the ocean and green leaves and everything else that constitutes our earthly home. Christina's mother had fulfilled a priestly role—priestly in the archetypal sense, in the priesthood of all believers—by allowing the child to participate in a daily ritual, a liturgy of the delicious orange, bright as the sun, sweet with the juice that is the body and blood of this world. The child who is thus fed by a mother's love eventually learns to trust in others, and also in God. The fruit we are given is not always what we expect or want; it may even be bitter, but we are secure in knowing that it is given to us out of love. The capacity for trust that begins in such ordinary human encounters, as between a mother and child, can come to have deep religious significance, not only for ourselves, but for the entire community of faith. As we come to know a God of limitless compassion, who has faith enough in us to make oranges, and life itself, "new every morning" (Lam 3:23), we can find great mercy even in the midst of lamentation. That lovely phrase, "new every morning," which I sometimes use as a koan on my customary walks at dawn, comes from the third Lamentation of Jeremiah. The prophet begins this lament with a terse statement: "I am one who has seen affliction," and continues with a grim description of his dire circumstances: "[God] has made my flesh and my skin waste away, and broken my bones; he has besieged and enveloped me with bitterness and tribulation; he has made me sit in darkness like the dead of long ago" (Lam 3:4–6).

The turning point comes for Jeremiah when he can recall the good that God has done, all the graces bestowed upon him and the people of Israel and all of creation: "But this I call to mind, and therefore I have hope: The steadfast love of the Lord never ceases, his mercies never come to an end; they are new every morning; great is your faithfulness" (Lam 3:21–23). Reminding ourselves that God's love for us is daily *and* everlasting can go a long way toward helping us live through the rough spots in our lives. And we also need the daily love of other people to reassure us that our lives have value. When we are too grieving, bitter or depressed to pray, they can pray for us and carry us along. And when we are able again to pray, we can pray for them.

This is why our praise of God, like the praise contained within Jeremiah's lament, is not private, not personal, but communal. This is why the play of hope and lamentation, despair and gratitude that is so central to the prophets and the psalms has not lost its relevance for us. When we pray, we pray out of our common condition, as reflected in the image of a weaned child in Psalm 131:

> Truly I have set my soul
> in silence and peace.
> A weaned child on its mother's breast.
> even so is my soul (Ps 131:2, GR)

which inspires the psalmist to cry out: "O Israel, hope in the Lord,/both now and forever" (Ps 131:3, GR).

Now. And forever. Together, as a people. That is all that is required of us by the quotidian mysteries. Or, as Psalm 61 expresses it, "So I will always praise your name and day after day fulfill my vows" (Ps 61: 9, GR), a line that usually causes me to add a mental caveat, in case God really is listening, "or *neglect* to fulfill them." Looking up the word *quotidian* in Eric Partridge's *Origins,* I am pointed to the realm of the holy, to the words *deus* (meaning "God") and *dies* (meaning "daylight" or "duration of a day"), which are closely related. They are both linked semantically in that, as Partridge writes, "the luminous sky...and daylight itself were apprehended as divine forces and manifestations," and phonetically, in the Indo-European root, meaning "to shine, be luminous." One definition of a god was "the shining one." The element *quot* brings the word *quotidian* down to earth, as it were, with more pedestrian concerns; it is concerned with quantity, as in how many days?

I have come to believe that the true mystics of the quotidian are not those who contemplate holiness in isolation, reaching godlike illumination in serene silence, but those who manage to find God in a life filled with noise, the demands of other people and relentless daily duties that can consume the self. They may be young parents juggling child-rearing and making a living; they may be monks or nuns in a small community who have to wear three or four "hats" because there are more jobs to fill than people to fill them. If they are wise, they treasure the rare moments of solitude and silence that come their way, and use them not to escape, to distract themselves with television and the like. Instead, they listen for a sign of God's presence and they open their hearts toward prayer.

And they recognize, as Gerard Manley Hopkins so eloquently stated it in a passage on the *Spiritual Exercises* of St. Ignatius Loyola, that

> It is not only prayer that gives God glory but work. Smiting on an anvil, sawing a beam, white-washing a wall, driving horses, sweeping, scouring, everything gives God some glory if being in His grace you do it as your duty. To go to communion worthily gives God

great glory, but to take food in thankfulness and temperance gives Him glory too. To lift up the hands in prayer gives God glory, but a man with a dungfork in his hand, a woman with a slop pail, give Him glory, too. God is so great that all things give Him glory if you mean that they should.

This is incarnational reality, the sanctity of the everyday. Yet, especially for women, such elevation of daily work has all too often proved condescending, too easy a means of keeping us in our place. Nowadays, when we hear lip service paid to "the women in the kitchen," it is often by men (and sometimes other women) who would not dream of carrying a dungfork or slop pail, let alone cook a meal, set a table or wash the dishes. The paradox remains, however, as these are essential tasks, and they retain possibilities for religious meaning. In addressing the paradox, allow me to employ a metaphor from religious life, and let me speak to you as a domestic or lay sister, and not a choir nun. It's not so far-fetched. Beyond a bachelor's degree in liberal arts, I have no other credentials except experience, reading and writing.

I recently reviewed a book entitled *Through the Kitchen Window* and was glad to consider its premise that the feminist movement had come of age to the extent that women might now feel free to speak about something as ordinary as cooking without being labeled traitors to the cause. I remember all too well the bad old days of the early 1970s, when one friend's "consciousness-raising" group, giddy with its new-found ideology, criticized her for having "nonfeminist" sofas. They were not strong sofas, as in Swedish modern, but small, velvet-upholstered sofas on dainty, highly polished legs. Worst of all, they were pastel pink and blue. And I recall an argument that ensued when I dared to read a poem about washing dishes; I inadvertently caused intelligent people to have a heated exchange about whether or not this sort of thing could only land women back in *Father Knows Best* territory. The only contribution I could make was to say that my poem didn't have much to do with the actual washing of dishes, but was about my husband and me talking late at night in our kitchen. It was about the building up of a relationship on the scary ground of marriage, which entails the daily dirtying and cleansing of dishes. But I didn't see any reason to post a warning label on the poem to notify potential readers that it was okay for me to be washing up at the kitchen sink, as my husband had cooked the meal.

Thus, I began reading the kitchen anthology with heightened expectations, and soon recognized my own adolescent self in the introduction by the editor, Arlene Voski Avakian. She admits that as a child in the 1950s, having sized up women's roles in her Armenian-American household, she decided that cooking was something she would refuse to do. This struck memory chords in me; seeking a life of the mind, I had more or less consciously rejected the "girl stuff" that I associated with my mother in her kitchen. Now I realize that this rejection of the sanctity of daily tasks was self-defeating in the long run. It served to alienate me not only from the wisdom of my mother and grandmothers, but from the pleasure of cooking, serving and eating some very good food.

I could see myself also in the provocative remarks of Ruth Hubbard, a feminist scientist whom the editor had approached as a possible contributor to this volume. At first Hubbard asks, peevishly, "Haven't we had enough of women being viewed through the kitchen window?" but then she offers a touching description of her own mother as being "of the generation of Central European women...who escaped the kitchen by becoming first a music teacher and then a physician." After some correspondence with the editor, Hubbard makes this telling remark: "I had never thought about the...obvious fact that preparing a meal can be a sign of caring and loving communication, because food just has never been an avenue of communication for me." I suspect that Hubbard's experience is not particularly feminist in nature, but reflects the preoccupation of many scientists, male and female, whose energies are often directed away from the hearth and into the library and the lab.

But her statement does reveal the dilemma that daily household tasks have become for women. Must we choose between a life of the mind and a life of repetitive, burdensome work? This dilemma is replicated in the anthology itself. I found it interesting that some of the contributors, mostly college professors, had to resort to the ponderous prose of academese in order to justify writing about the lowly kitchen arts. Two examples might suffice:

I am deeply driven by creative forces and subterranean needs that have found the preparation of just the right meal the most compelling form of expression.

...what do I make of my mother's deconstruction of her own recipes? Do I stick to the text itself, making the recipe as written and respecting its independent and autonomous authority, or do I follow my mother's emendations, participate with her in her guerilla attack on the recipe's textual authority?

Other writers found fresher ways to express the humble mystery of an inherited recipe. Here is Ketu H. Katrak, an East Indian scholar and poet, who says it in simple English:

A recipe has so many different hands and minds in its history—I cannot recall who taught me what, and what parts I invented.

That's the boundaryless pleasure of cooking; no one authorship. What counts is the final taste.

I imagine that the cooking of food is a lot like laundry. It is not normally considered a proper subject for conversation, particularly among intellectuals, but if you start asking around, you will find that people take it much more personally than you might imagine. Avakian's book contains memorable portraits of women that I suspect we all can picture, such as Julie Dash's great-aunt Gertie. Dash writes that if she "had lived long enough to see rice in a perforated plastic bag being tossed around a pot of boiling water—she would not have lived to the age of ninety-three."

A mature feminism recognizes that subjects such as cooking can be difficult for women to address, as they have so often been seen as insignificant "women's work," but it also asks us to recognize that their intimate nature makes them serious and important. Many of us might resonate with Leah Ryan's comment, "When I was growing up, food was the closest thing our household had to a religion," and also with Gloria Wade-Gayles's summing-up of what does not need translating, the universal gift of basic, wholesome cooking, no matter who is doing it: "I'd swear Mama put some good juju in her food."

Reading Avakian's anthology, I recalled the

tender subterfuge that my grandfather Norris employed; by convincing my grandmother that store-bought bread was bad for his stomach, he got her to keep baking her own. Which she loved to do, of course. Both of my grandmothers took justifiable pride in the quality of their homemade bread and the way we grandkids would savor it when we visited in the summer. I can still recall its texture: chewy, but also impossibly light. All I could think of was to ask for more. For nearly twenty-five years, half of my life, I have inhabited the kitchen of my grandmother Totten, and am convinced that it was her spirit that inspired me to learn to bake bread when I moved from New York City in 1974. Baking bread is only one of the experiences that I took on in her house and small town, and it made me a better-grounded person, more in touch with the real world, and allowed me to cast off the aimless and overly cerebral young woman that I had become.

Laundry, liturgy and women's work all serve to ground us in the world, and they need not grind us down. Our daily tasks, whether we perceive them as drudgery or essential, life-supporting work, do not define who we are as women or as human beings. But they have a considerable spiritual import, and their significance for Christian theology, the way they come together in the fabric of faith, is not often appreciated. But it is daily tasks, daily acts of love and worship that serve to remind us that the religion is not strictly an intellectual pursuit, and these days it is easy to lose sight of that as, like our society itself, churches are becoming more politicized and polarized. Christian faith is a way of life, not an impregnable fortress made up of ideas; not a philosophy; not a grocery list of beliefs.

The Christian creeds used to seem like a "grocery list" to me, and I found them very difficult to incorporate into my fledgling faith, as I made my way back to church after twenty years away. But now I see them as an admirably compact form of storytelling, and this makes me glad, for story places the creeds in the realm of the daily. It is in ordinary life that our stories unfold, tales of conceiving, bearing and giving birth, of trial and death and rising to new life out of the ashes of the old. Stories of annunciation, incarnation, resurrection, and the spirit, the giver of life, who has spoken through the prophets and enlivens our faith. As wondrous as these mysteries are, Christianity is inescapably down-to-earth and incarnational—I say "inescapably," as most of us, at one time or another, try to avoid the implications of an incarnational faith. The Christian religion asks us to place our trust not in ideas, and certainly not in ideologies, but in a God who was vulnerable enough to become human and die, and who desires to be present to us in our everyday circumstances. And because we are human, it is in the realm of the daily and the mundane that we must find our way to God.

Teresa of Avila implies in her *Autobiography* that it is through other people that God chooses to reach out to us. "If Christ Jesus dwells in us..." she writes, "then we can endure all things, for Christ helps and strengthens us and never abandons us. He is a true friend. And I clearly see that if we expect to please him and receive an abundance of his graces, God desires that these graces must come to us from the hands of Christ, through his most sacred humanity, in which God takes delight." In our life of faith, then, as well as in our most intimate relationships with other people, our task is to transform the high romance of conversion, the fervor of a religious call, into daily commitment. Into the sort of friendship that transcends infatuation and can endure all things. Our desire is to love God and each other, in stable relationships that, like any good marriage, remain open to surprises and receptive to grace.

Human beings need routine. Even the homeless, I have been told by those who minister to them, establish routine as best they can, walking the same streets, foraging in the same dumpsters, sleeping in the same spots, in an attempt to maintain basic relationships with people and places. In this sense routine can be a lifesaver. But especially for those of us who have more material wealth, it can also be a depressant, a killer. People grow bored with their marriages and their jobs, their coworkers and their spouses. I have long suspected that much of the self-destructive behavior and even the suicides of people who seem to have all that anyone could want, are the result of sheer exhaustion, the inability to continue in the daily round of getting more. Airplane travel can be instructive in this regard: if you want to know what is really going on in the American corporate world, spend some time listening to a young businesswoman in the seat next to you tell what it is like to feel pressured to work ninety hours a week as she also tries to be a good wife and mother. Or hear the anguish of a man in his early fifties, deemed obsolete by the company where he has worked for nearly thirty years. He has spent an entire year resisting attempts to make him quit his job before his pension would kick in. His daily routine has become a torment; there is no longer anyone among his colleagues at work that he feels he can trust. He says that his marriage and two children have been his salvation, and while he still worries about providing for his family, he has found that their unconditional love, even the children's desire to play with him when he comes home from work, is enough to get him through the day. This has sanctified his marriage and his life at a time when in most of his waking hours he has been made to feel worthless.

Ironically, it seems that it is by the means of seemingly perfunctory daily rituals and routines that we enhance the personal relationships that nourish and sustain us. I read recently, in Martin Marty's newsletter, "Context," of a study that monitored the habits of married couples in order to determine what made for good marriages. The researchers found that only one activity seemed to make a consistent difference, in terms of the ability to maintain a stable, happy, long-lasting relationship, and that was simple affection, the embracing or kissing of one's spouse at the beginning and the end of each workday.

Most significantly, as Paul Bosch, the author of the article reports, "it didn't seem to matter whether or not in that moment the partners were fully 'engaged' or even sincere! Just a perfunctory peck on the cheek seemed to be enough—enough to make a difference in the quality of the relationship!" Bosch comments, wisely, that this "should not surprise churchgoers. Whatever you do repeatedly," he writes, "has the power to shape you, has the power to make you over into a different person— even if you're not totally 'engaged' in every minute!"

I wonder if we might substitute that "peck on the cheek" for some of the prayers that a religious community recites daily: the Doxology, the Lord's

Prayer, the Benedictus at lauds and the Magnificat at vespers. No human being can pay full attention to the words that he or she is praying every single day, and apparently this is how God would have it. Sometimes, particularly at crisis points in our lives, we feel these words with our whole heart. They seem to burn in our chests, and bring tears to our eyes. We find that we mean them in ways that remain unfathomable, and on rare occasions a new interpretation of a line or image will come to us. I will never forget the day I realized that the "you, child" of the Benedictus could refer not only to John the Baptist but to myself, and to any of us who know that we are asked "to go before the Lord to prepare the way." That morning, and every morning that I pray this poem, I receive a challenge, whether I consciously acknowledge it or not, and an image of holiness to strive for. I am asked to share with others "the tender compassion of God" as it breaks like the dawn upon us. I am asked to cast its light "on those who dwell in the shadow of death," and allow my feet to be guided, this day, and all days, "into the way of peace" (Lk 1:76, 78, 79, ELLC).

Similarly, the Magnificat summons me to hope, at the end of each day, a hope that there is an alternative to the world I have been working in. A world in which I can address God, saying "You have shown strength with your arm,/and scattered the proud in their schemes" (Lk 1:51, ELLC), a world

in which the rich will come to know their emptiness and the hungry will be filled. But all too
often, I pray these two magnificent prayers with
only half a mind, one half yawning, only dimly conscious that it is praying, and the other half dwelling
on the fact that my feet hurt and I might consider
buying new shoes—perhaps even imagining their
color and style—or worse, I mentally linger over
some petty slight, working up an anger that dis-
tracts me from prayer. As for the words that I am
dutifully saying, I might as well be praying in
tongues, and maybe I am. And maybe the prayer is
working despite myself.

It is a paradox of human life that in worship, as
in human love, it is in the routine and the everyday that we find the possibilities for the greatest
transformation. Both worship and housework
often seem perfunctory. And both, by the grace
of God, may be anything but. At its Latin root,
perfunctory means "to get through with," and we
can easily see how liturgy, laundry and what has
traditionally been conceived of as "women's
work" can be done in that indifferent spirit. But
the joke is on us: what we think we are only "getting through" has the power to change us, just as
we have the power to transform what seems
meaningless—the endless repetitions of a litany or
the motions of vacuuming a floor. What we dread
as mindless activity can free us, mind and heart,
for the workings of the Holy Spirit, and repetitive

motions are conducive to devotions such as the Jesus Prayer or the rosary. Anything is fair game for prayer, anything or anyone who pops into the mind can be included.

One prayer that I treasure, no matter what I am engaged in, comes from the great lyricist Isaac Watts in his rendition of Psalm 23, entitled, "My Shepherd Will Supply My Need." Watts interprets the ending of the psalm—"Surely goodness and kindness shall follow me all the days of my life. In the Lord's own house shall I dwell forever and ever" (Ps 22:6, GR)—not as some future event, but as existing in the light of the present, the every-day. Watts writes: "The sure provisions of my God/Attend me all my days. O may thy house be my abode/And all my work be praise!"

To convert all our work into prayer and praise is admittedly an ideal, but the contemplatives of the world's religions might agree that it is something to strive for. I once saw a photograph of a Buddhist nun sweeping a temple floor with a smile that was as peaceful and wise as that of the Buddha. With her whole body she exemplified the grace of that connection between prayer and work that is so much a part of the Benedictine tradition. When I recently conducted a weekend retreat at a monastery, I was pleasantly surprised to find that a third of the participants were health care workers—registered nurses, nursing home attendants and hospice volunteers—who had recognized their

need for a break from their stressful work.
Through our silence and conversation, our contemplation and storytelling, it became clear that
they also knew that in a hospital or hospice room,
where people need assistance with the most basic
of tasks—breathing, eating, urinating, excreting
and bathing—the holiness of ordinary acts is made
most manifest. It is there, at one extreme of
human vulnerability, that we come to realize that
all we customarily take for granted is truly a gift
from God. The Christian faith also asks us to
acknowledge that to shortchange these quotidian
gifts is to reject God's incarnation in Jesus Christ.

We are, all of us, Christian women and men,
engaged in priestly work, the work of transformation. But it may be work that is deemed useless by
the standards of the world. Bathing a woman who
is in a coma, for example, a woman many would
say is better off dead. The poet Laura Gilpin, who
is a nurse, has a poem entitled "The Bath" that
quietly reflects on such an experience:

> I stand here bathing her
> while she sleeps
> in a far place beyond my reaching.
>
> I bathe her
> as I have been taught to do:
> first the eyes, then the forehead,
> the face, the neck.

The poet talks to the woman all the while, "believing that hearing is the last to go," but is not certain that her words have any effect. The poem (and I believe it is a prayer) concludes:

> She offers no resistance,
> except that of gravity,
> the earth pulling her down
> while I lift,
> as though something between us
> is being weighed.
>
> Then I turn her to wash her back
> talking to her about what seems to matter
> in this life—though I make no promises.
>
> Only this morning
> the promise of spring was in the air
> and I tell her that.

We are asked to make all that we have been taught and trained to do—as nurses, educators, theologians, poets, doctors, secretaries, accountants or what-have-you—available to God. Especially when human need is at its greatest, and we know ourselves to be incapable of meeting that need on our own, we are asked to find our strength in Jesus Christ. And we are asked to make our most serious and intimate commitments with very little idea of how long they will last, or what will be required of us. The ordinary demands of a pregnancy, for example, require a woman to find the strength to give birth to a child who, even if it is healthy, will need daily nurturing for years, who will most likely devalue and rebel against that nurture in adolescence, and who will eventually leave home for schooling, work and a marriage of her own. At the deepest level, a pregnant woman must find the courage to give birth to a creature who will one day die, as she herself must die. And there are no promises, other than the love of God, to tell us that this human round is anything but futile.

In one of my poems, "Ascension," I tried to restore a sense of gravity and beauty to the image of a mother and infant, which is often sentimentalized in our culture. I wrote the poem because of a simple juxtaposition in my life. On Ascension one year, my mother phoned to tell me that my sister's water had broken and she had gone to the hospital to have her second child. And all day I couldn't get the thought out of my mind that as Jesus was rising to heaven, my sister was pushing down for all she was worth. Here is the poem that resulted from that meditation:

ASCENSION

Why do you stand looking up at the sky?–Acts 1:11

It wasn't just wind chasing
thin, gunmetal clouds

across a loud sky.
And it wasn't the feeling that one might
      ascend
on that excited air,
rising like a trumpet note,

and it wasn't just my sister's water breaking,
her crying out,
the downward draw of blood and bone....

It was all of that,
mud and new grass
pushing up through melting snow,
the lilac in bud by my front door
bent low
by last week's ice storm.

Now the new mother, that leaky vessel,
begins to nurse her child,
beginning the long good-bye.

And in another poem, a new one named for the
hot lunch program for the elderly in my small
town, I pay homage to the other end of life. Here
is "Nutrition Site":

We are off-site now,
in the van, delivering
hot meals
in a fierce winter.
One widow's house

87

smells of stale water.
Ancient linoleum peels
and buckles
on the wounded
hardwood floor.

Her Valentine roses
have lost their bloom;
wrinkled, they droop
on their stems,
as if weighted
by beauty.

Their beauty. Yes.
Like the widow's icy walk,
her gnarled hand
on the lap
robe, in the musty
living room, her Bible
open to Isaiah 35:
"and the desert shall rejoice,
and blossom as the rose,"

her wrinkly smile
as I knock and
enter. Beauty, yes. All of it.
And truth.

REFERENCES:

Gibson, Margaret. "Making Salad." *Out in the Open*. (Baton Rouge: Louisiana State University Press, 1989).

Gilpin, Laura. "The Bath." *Poetry* (May 1984).

Norris, Kathleen. "Housecleaning," "Persephone," "Ascension." *Little Girls in Church*. (Pittsburgh: University of Pittsburgh Press, 1995).

———. "Nutrition Site." unpublished poem.

Porter, Anne. "An Easter Lily." *An Altogether Different Language*. (Cambridge MA: Zoland Books, 1994).

ABBREVIATIONS FOR BIBLICAL TRANSLATIONS:

Biblical quotations are from the New Revised Standard Version, except where noted.

KJV—King James Version.

ELLC—English Language Liturgical Commission, 1988.

GR—The Grail (England), 1993.

The Madeleva Lecture in Spirituality

This series, sponsored by the Center for Spirituality, Saint Mary's College, Notre Dame, Indiana, honors annually the woman who as president of the college inaugurated its pioneering graduate program in theology, Sister M. Madeleva, C.S.C.

1985
Monika K. Hellwig
Christian Women in a Troubled World

1986
Sandra M. Schneiders
Women and the Word

1987
Mary Collins
Women at Prayer

1988
Maria Harris
Women and Teaching

1989
Elizabeth Dreyer
Passionate Women: Two Medieval Mystics

1990
Joan Chittister
Job's Daughters

1991
Dolores R. Leckey
Women and Creativity

1992
Lisa Sowle Cahill
Women and Sexuality

1993
Elizabeth A. Johnson
Women, Earth and Creator Spirit

1994
Gail Porter Mandell
Madeleva: One Woman's Life

1995
Diana L. Hayes
Hagar's Daughters

1996
Jeanette Rodriguez
Stories We Live
Cuentos Que Vivimos

1997
Mary C. Boys
Jewish-Christian Dialogue
One Woman's Experience